T0068186

GODLY VERSES

JERRY WARREN

iUniverse

GODLY VERSES

iUniverse books may be ordered through booksellers or by contacting:

iUniverse
1663 Liberty Drive
Bloomington, IN 47403
www.iuniverse.com
844-349-9409

ISBN: 978-1-6632-5635-5 (sc)
ISBN: 978-1-6632-5636-2 (e)

Library of Congress Control Number: 2023917594

Print information available on the last page.

iUniverse rev. date: 09/21/2023

THIS BOOK IS DEDICATED TO
A HOLY ENTITY COMMONLY KNOWN AS
TO THE HOLY TRINITY

Perfection

On a cross, Jesus was nailed
With His blood, sin is repelled
Perfection is sacrificed
With His blood were sanctified
Without His blood, the world will have failed

Good/Evil

Good is always there
Goodness ready to share
Evil will always malign
Is there any evil that is kind?
God's love is good for soul repair

Trust/Faith

In God I will try to trust
Along with faith it is a must
With faith in God, we live
My tithes I will freely give
God is perfectly just

Conception

When does life begin?
There is that question again
That debate is ongoing
Abortion rights is growing
Spilling innocent blood, is sin

Prayer

To God my creator I pray
My gratitude is hard to relay
My prayer, the holy spirit will align
That will make my prayer divine
And God will bless me each day

God

He is always with us
Amid all turmoil and fuss
Each person has their own
Depends on what seed is sown
The true God's son is Jesus

Trust

Trust God, not man
Do this whenever you can
Man will let you down
Faith in man is not sound
With God I will always stand

Backbone

A building needs a foundation
Our soul and spirit need is salvation
The backbone of the church is Jesus
Just remember, He watches over us
With Jesus we need to form a
spiritual relation

God's Blessing

All blessings are in God's port
Will any be issued to those who abort?
The supreme court did amend
A baby's life they want to defend
Will God withdraw His support?

Who Gains

Of what will anyone gain
If abortion is cause of blame
It may free someone up
To drink from the evil cup
Do none of it in God's name

Eternity

A place where God resides
A place where only God decides
Where time does not exist
There is no sin to resist
Where there is nobody who derides

Sin

Sin, is what all are guilty of
He observes us from above
There is only one way to win
Only one who can forgive sin
The one who forgives with love

Moment

A moment is a measure
In a life of sorrow or pleasure
In heaven, moments do not consist
There, time does not exist
A moment with God, is what I treasure

Value

On life, can you place value?
Whether, it is old or new
There's value in potential
But for this, life is essential
Who placed value on just a few?

Goals

By people some goals are set
Most people will soon forget
Seeking God is a good endeavor
To try to be with Him forever
A goal you will not regret

Middle Ground

There is no middle ground
In this world, sin is not bound
One should listen to God's voice
Until death you have a choice
For hell, or to where no sin is found

Blood

Blood is what is needed
For sin to be defeated
Blood of the Lamb
Under His blood we stand
And salvation is completed

Positive

A positive realization
Is found in most situations
Develop a positive trend
With Christ unto your end
God is my positive inspiration

Word

I bet that you have heard
In the beginning was the word
Flesh the word became
Jesus Christ is His name
With Him, Salvation is at your curb

Humility/Pride

Give glory to God in all good you do
Pray each day for God to guide you through
Pride will cause many to go their own way
They'll not listen to what God has to say
To God we should always stay true

Confidence

Where does confidence come from
I will credit mine to the Son
With Him all is possible
And He is very reliable
To follow Him can be hard but fun

Reminder

We all have a reminder
That it is God's creation we live under
It's His creation where we exist
His authority, do not resist
He reminds us, sin is to Him our asunder

Vacuum

Of God a nation is empty for all to see
Evil spirits will not let this be
Our creator should not be denied
This nation has certainly tried
Accept Jesus and follow Him to be set free
A Godless nation pays the evil darkness fee

Jesus

Jesus is God and savior
He is also the Son and creator
We are the branch, He is the vine
With Him we want to entwine
In Jesus, we are His debtor

Vision

A sight that is unseen
The minds eye in a dream
Always keep God in your vision
With Him should be no confusion
God is the answer, all should Him is high esteem

Spectator

In a game there are players
Then there are the watchers
There are those who want to win
To do this they must defeat sin
For God, do not be a Sunday spectator

Remainder

After all is said and done
Nothing left except the Son
In the beginning He was there
His church is in His care
The remainder is the Trinity and then none

Struggle

Struggles we all will face
Belief fractured by the living pace
Slow down for God is always around
God's word is very sound
Our heavenly goal is not a race

Trust

Friendship is built on trust
For a relationship, this is a must
God trusts us to do what is right
Even when your out of others sight
Without trust, friendship will tarnish and rust

Forgive

Forgive and forget is God's way
Listen to all He has to say
Love and forgiveness go hand in hand
And this is where we should stand
All should let God be their sway

Altar

What will you sacrifice on this altar of life
Can your lifestyle us a proverbial knife
A behavioral change is usually required
When seeking God is most desired
Prayer will guide you through a much strife

Influence

Do not try to influence others
Let your actions influence sisters and brothers
The right thing you should always do
Even when nobody is watching you
Live your life influenced by the, Father

Chasten/Disciplinary

Inside you the spirit has come
You have accepted the, Son
For their sin, the Saved will be chastened
Until their walk back to Good is hastened
To this world and sin, do not succumb

Christianity

In Christ, there are believers
The devil also has his deceivers
Toward God, some will lean
His word they daily glean
Christians are the Christ receivers

Trends

Is Christianity this months trend?
Then with God, you do not stand
Do not be a Christian pretender
Instead, be a Christ defender
With Christ, become a friend

Sideline

Along the side is where you are
Staying there you'll not go far
With God you need to stay connected
For you could be the one selected
Follow Jesus, He will become your
Guiding star

Fiction Christian

In worship to God, don't be fictitious
Of God always be conscious
Lip service God does not deserve
Give God your heart without reserve
We depend on God being very gracious

Jesus

For our sin, He was crucified
On a cross, perfection died
To the Father, for us, He represents
So, to be saved each truly repents
And be baptized is for each to decide

End of Days

End of days is very near
The wrath of God I fear
Accept Jesus as your savior
You may need to change behavior
For you, God does truly care

Life

It seems that life hangs by a thread
To die, the conscious mind may dread
Life eternal is what I desire
With my God, that I love and admire
I believe the promises of what God has said

Enemy

The enemy is at your gate
He is full of lies and hate
Do not let Him inside
In your heart let God abide
Only with God should we relate

Prolife

Avoid abortion if you can
Prolife is where I stand
Abortion is a shameful sin
It is between God and them
Repent and get right with God again

Repentance

Baptize and repent
Accept the one God sent
He is the worlds, savior
We should try to copy His behavior
The world awaits, for Jesus to descend

Word to Flesh

I bet that you have heard
That God in flesh came from the word
The Word caused the creation
With man He starts a relation
All but Christians, find this absurd

Disciple

We all have a choice
To follow and listen to His voice
Become a follower of Jesus
From our sin He relieves us
Jesus gives us reason to rejoice

Creation

Some people have not believed
From sin they will not be relieved
They will not accept creation
With God, they have no relation
They will not believe a virgin did conceive

Honest

Being honest is the best way
A need to have people believe what I say
Being honest can be contentious
Especially among the religious
Honesty keeps the devil at bay

Fall

How great is the fall of man
When with God, they will not stand
Separated from God by our sin
The worst thing since the world begin
More than repentance, God does demand

Virtue

A high moral standard is virtue
Before God your life in review
Jesus, we try to emulate
So, with Jesus we can relate
With God, always be true

Bible

God wrote a book
For wisdom this is where to look
God's word is the holy bible
Some think it is a fable
Israel, God has not, forsook

Rational

There is sin, when God's law is broken
Psychically or maybe spoken
Sin, we should not rationalize
God's law, one cannot disguise
To follow God, be driven

New People

Christians are born again
A new life to begin
A new people are created
Psalms 102:18 is related
It's Jesus blood that cleansed their sin

Faith

A belief that is very strong
A belief that may be very wrong
With all my heart in God I believe
Accept His Son, eternal life you receive
With them I want to belong

Church

People are what make a church
Christians put the creator on a perch
Religion does not make a Christian
Without Christ their all fiction
For the creator, many will fail the search

Mind The Mind

To try with all my might
My mind is not always right
God needs to be in each moment
With Him, I find contentment
Act to bring joy into God's sight

Submission

To His love, I totally submit
Without His love, I would remit
Love is the center of creation
Love is the key to a successful relation
Truth and love, is what God into heaven
will admit

Principles

We live by our principles
They may be as warm as an icicle
Truthful is the way to live
Through God is the way to give
Live as a Christ disciple

Peace

What we all look for
When trouble knocks at our door
Peace, what I most desire
May be found when from this life I retire
And live with God forevermore

Risen

Jesus arose from the dead
On day three, death was shed
He is risen, is what they say
Back to life on the third day
Accept Jesus and defeat the death you dread

Focus

On Christ I will keep my eye
The Holy Spirit, I'll not deny
Like a laser, I focus
My mind is on Jesus
For only on Him, can I rely

Redemption

Accept Jesus and be saved
To Satan, some have caved
Repent and be redeemed
God, one should never demean
You should never act depraved

Delusion

Lie to yourself, about the way to go
The truth is, you don't want to know
Living in a delusion
A life with much confusion
To hell, you may very well go

Authority

Free will is what was given
To decide on how were living
To God give up your free will
For God, this world, one should repeal
For God my tithe I'm giving

Saved

Have you been saved?
Or are you depraved?
With Jesus I try to walk
To Him in prayer I daily talk
Darkness to light, with His blood
The road is paved.

Sanctified

Holy most anyone will become
When they truly follow the, Son
Through Jesus we are sanctified
With His blood, sin is nullified
Follow Jesus, He is the One

Pleasing

To please God, is hard to do
The path to Him is found by few
Accept Jesus, repent be baptized and proceed
For you, Jesus will intercede
Free from sin, we are made anew

Defence

Our help God does not need
He wants us to plant and water the seed
Our faith in Him is much appreciated
My love for Him has not abated
Through Jesus, from sin we are freed

Devotion

To whom or what are you devoted?
Is it material or spiritual related?
To this world, don't be devout
God is what it is all about
What we can and cannot see, He created

Truth

Truth is what Christian church stands for
Christ will change how you felt before
The truth will set you free
Truth will forever be
Truth and Jesus is at the Christian core.

Lost

You feel like you are lost
Away from God is the cost
To Him you should submit
Into His kingdom, you He may admit
With God, you should feel embossed

Revenge

Don't try to even the score
To them don't do any more
Revenge is in God's domain
A human it could drive insane
For Christians, love and forgiveness
Is the core

Mirror

Ten commandments God gave us
Follow these and learn to trust
Let these mirror your life's action
In God you'll have satisfaction
So, love God and follow Jesus

Spikes

In this world I have spikes of pleasure
Briefly here, hard to measure
God's love is not a spike
His unmeasurable love is what I like
My loving God, is my treasure

Place

We all need a place
To break from the living pace
Some find a place in their mind
Although there are many places of a different kind
Pray to God and thank Him for His grace

Prayer

On my knees I sometime pray
Kneeling, sitting, standing, God listens to what I say
To God goes honor and praise
On His face I pray to gaze
I want to be with God in heaven someday

Lonely

I know what it's like
It can mess with your psyche
To feel like you are in a shroud
By yourself when in a crowd
I pray to God give me His light

Cleave

To what do you cleave?
In Jesus you should believe
Old habits sit aside
With God you should abide
Through His blood, salvation you receive

His Will

God's will is to be done
In heaven and under the sun
He controls all of creation
With God we need a relation
Follow Him, it can be hard but fun

Devoted

To what are you devoted by name?
Money, sex, drugs, or fame
If to God you are devoted
Your faith in Him is well noted
Some will not play in His game

Slave

To what are you a slave?
To things of this world, you cave
Do not be a slave to sin
Keep your eyes and mind on Him
Like Jesus always try to behave

Clock

Our life is on a clock
Your life's boat will soon dock
You leave the boat to go ashore
Heaven or Hell, do you care?
Will Satan block you from Jesus flock?

Light

When you walk in the light
You will always try to do right
In the dark you will lose your way
When you are not under Gods sway
Always keep God in sight

Abide

Surrender to Jesus in every way
Heed His word every day
The devil will tempt you
Cause you to question all that you do
Don't forget, God is in you to stay

Gift

There are many gifts given
Issued to us while were living
The Holy Spirit is in us all
Which gifts to us is His call
To please God, we should be driven

King

Oh, to Him I will sing
I want the joy He will bring
I will go where He does lead
On His word I will feed
Jesus Christ is my king

Doubt

Praise God with a shout
When in God, you have doubt
Jesus is the creator
We should be His imitator
Jesus is what it is all about

Glory

All glory God should get
Even though it has not occurred yet
All the good that you do
Is Christ working through you
Live like this, with no regret

Resurrection

Being raised from the dead
Deaths, sting has been shed
Christ died for you and me
From sin He set us free
So, my death I do not dread

Fire

For what are you on fire?
What/whom do you most admire?
Jesus can be a major part
If you let Him into your heart
He will become the fire of your desire

Guide

We all need a spiritual guide
To help us to decide
By faith we should believe
That a virgin did conceive
In Jesus we should confide and abide

Universe

Everything is in its place
All is moving at the right pace
The universe is not in chaos
For God is still the boss
If He loosens His grip, we are erased

Donation

To what or whom do you donate?
For some, giving is a natural trait
Giving for/to God is best
This practice some detest
Giving in Gods name could determine your fate

Justify

Actions, some try to justify
On their own understanding they rely
Ask God about what to do
When a false charge is against you
Seek the Lord, His counsel, do not deny

Light

Seek Him, walk in His light
With Jesus you will find much delight
Repent in Christ be born anew
The Holy Spirit is in you
In you, let His light shine bright

Treasure

When living for God is your pleasure
That is right by any measure
Value is revealed by the heart
Hopefully God is the main part
For therein lies your treasure

Living Water

Water, we cannot live without
Life giving water is what it is all about
Living water is salvation from Jesus
Through the Holy Spirit He knows us
To the Father, Jesus, and Holy Spirit be devout

Dreams

Dreams is what some live for
Maybe it is behind the very next door
Maybe your dream is of gold
Dreams may cause one to act bold
Your dreams should have God at the core

Submit

To who do you willingly submit?
To all do you proudly admit?
Jesus should be the one
He is Gods only Son
To follow Him, do you remit, or commit?

Please

Who do you want to please?
Certain ones we should not tease
Jesus is the only one
Gods one and only Son
Obedience, to them we should appease

Entrance

Around, some people will prance
Wanting to make a grand entrance
In them God is missing
They will not receive a blessing
Against God they take a stance

Joy

True joy you will emit
When to Jesus you submit
You can go to any length
When joy of the Lord is your strength
Then into Heaven, you He will admit

Attitude

An attitude is so important
To do things without resentment
Gratitude should be shown
For all good to you is known
Through Jesus you can find contentment

Answer

Questions, there is a lot
Answers, are still sought
God is the Father of one
Jesus Christ is His Son
This the Holy Spirit taught

Idol

Whom do you idolize?
Who do you demonize?
Father God, your idol should be
Accept His Son, and salvation is free
Through them eternal life you will realize

Believe

In Jesus, do you believe
That a virgin did conceive
Virgin birth and resurrection
Bible written by Gods recollection
Gods promise will not deceive

Happiness

Being happy is a frame of mind
May result from being kind
In Gods, name do good
Act right as you always should
Follow Jesus and these attributes you will find

Comprpmise

Sin, do not rationalize
For God has no compromise
Repent when law is broken
Pay by prayer, not by token
Forgiveness, you will realize

Journey

Life is a journey, not a trip
Lifes voyage is not a radar blip
Heaven is my destination
Jesus is my salvation
Into living water my cup, I will dip

Test

Every day there is a test
Which path for me is best
Christians know the way
All should walk that path every day
By Father God, you will be blest

Fate

What will be your fate?
Is it up for debate?
Predestination is in play
Determines what you do each day
If with Jesus you relate

Repent

With you, God is not content
That is a time for you to repent
Sincerity and remorse must be shown
To remove the sin, you have sown
Could help to elude eternal torment

Forgive

To forgive and forget
Your sin God will remit
When to God you repent
Accept Jesus and be content
Your life to Jesus, you should commit

Printed in the United States
by Baker & Taylor Publisher Services